AI in Cyber Insurance
Risk Assessments and Coverage Decisions

Table of Contents

Chapter 1. Introduction

Welcome to this exclusive Special Report – 'AI in Cyber Insurance: Risk Assessments and Coverage Decisions.' Positioned in the fascinating cross-section between technology and finance, this report takes a considerate approach to sharing insights on a highly complex but increasingly significant area. In a world experiencing an exponential rise in cyber threats, understanding the role of Artificial Intelligence (AI) in shaping cyber insurance nuances is of paramount importance. Delving into an in-depth analysis on AI's sophisticated methodologies in risk assessments, and exploring its potential impacts on coverage decisions, this report simplifies the convoluted to the accessible. Here's your chance to navigate the labyrinth of AI in cyber insurance with ease and confidence. Don't let the technical nature deter you; we've crafted this Special Report to appeal to both seasoned techie and curious novice alike. So buckle up and join us on this enlightening journey, where clarity, understanding, and knowledge are the prime destinations.

Chapter 2. Understanding Cyber Insurance: An Overview

Cyber Insurance, also known as cyber liability insurance, is a modern kind of coverage that helps organizations mitigate financial losses associated with cyber threats and attacks. As we increasingly move into the digital era, almost all industries and sectors are heavily reliant on IT infrastructure, making them vulnerable to a wide range of cyber risks.

Before we venture ahead, it's essential to understand the type of events that may trigger a cyber insurance policy. These typically include, but aren't limited to, unauthorized access, cases of data breach, ransomware attacks, business email compromise, social engineering threats, and network damage.

2.1. Anatomy of a Cyber Insurance Policy

Every policy consists of several coverages that revolve around first-party and third-party perils.

First-party coverages generally include incident response services (forensic investigations, legal advice, notification costs, etc.), business interruption losses, digital asset restoration costs, cyber extortion payments and PR management expenditure. The aim is to offer immediate response mechanisms and measures to limit the attack's impact, minimize downtime, and offer crisis management solutions.

In contrast, third-party coverages protect against claims filed against the insured by customers, clients, or other entities for failure in securing sensitive information. It includes network security and privacy liability, regulatory fines and penalties coverage, media liability coverage, and network security liability.

2.2. Risk Assessment in Cyber Insurance

Risk assessment is a vital segment of any insurance procedure, more so in the case of cyber insurance due to the dynamic nature of cyber threats. It involves the following steps:

1. Identifying potential cyber risks associated with a company, its operations, and its defenses against cyber threats.

2. Understanding the impact of these risks on different aspects of the business, including financial, operational, reputational, and legal elements.

3. Prioritizing the risks based on their potential impact and likelihood of occurrence.

Additionally, insurers value continuous, proactive monitoring for cyber threats to ensure more accurate risk assessments and enforce protective measures.

2.3. Cyber Insurance – Premium Calculation

Premium calculation for cyber insurance is a complex process as it balances numerous factors like the insurer's size, nature of business, revenue, cybersecurity posture, claim history, and deductibles. Insurers also consider the organization industry's risk profile. For example, a healthcare or finance company, known for managing vast personal data, may have higher premiums than a manufacturing company.

Despite the sophistication, critics often pinpoint a lack of standardized methodology in premium calculation, thus making it subjective and inconsistent. However, the industry is continually evolving, thanks to advancements in AI and Big Data, to offer uniform premium guidelines.

2.4. Cyber Insurance Limitations

While exceedingly beneficial, cyber insurance does come with its limitations. Specifically, certain perils might fall outside standard coverage, such as:

1. Unquantifiable reputational damages
2. Costs associated with improving internal technology systems post-incident
3. Losses from an un-insured policy's exclusion (such as IP theft)

Moreover, the lack of long-term historical data makes accurate pricing and risk assessment challenging for insurers.

2.5. The Role and Impact of Regulations

Regulations play a substantial role in the shaping of the cyber insurance market. Ever-evolving regulatory requirements, such as GDPR in Europe and CCPA in California, which impose steep penalties in the event of data breaches, create an environment where cyber insurance becomes even more vital for businesses.

These regulations influence the demand for cyber insurance and act as drivers for more broad-ranging and inclusive policies. Compliance with the evolving regulatory landscape is set to continue as a major consideration for both insurers and businesses in the future.

2.6. Cyber Insurance Market Trends

The current market trends include increasing cyber threats and attacks, advancement in technology, regulatory changes and growing awareness about cyber risks. These have led to a marked expansion in the cyber insurance market.

Increasing number of businesses are opting for cyber insurance to ward off potential financial liabilities. As such, insurers are continuously developing diverse cyber coverages to cater to the ever-evolving cyber risks.

To address these needs, AI is likely to play a crucial role in improving risk assessments, policy pricing, underwriting efficiency, claim management, and fraud detection. The infusion of AI-driven methodologies in cyber insurance signifies an enlightening era of data-backed decision-making and enhanced customer services.

In conclusion, understanding cyber insurance is not a one-time effort. It demands ongoing vigilance and adaptation to an ever-changing cyber landscape. The use AI and advanced technologies is aiding this process, promising more accurate risk assessments, comprehensive coverage, and equitable pricing. This bodes well for the future, indicating not only developmental strides for the insurance industry, but for organizations' fight against cyber risk too.

Chapter 3. The Role of AI in Today's Digital Economy

Artificial Intelligence (AI) is profoundly redefining the digital economy. Its ongoing integration demonstrates a remarkable ability to deliver optimized business performance and foster innovation, while equally presenting complex challenges and risks.

3.1. Driving Innovation and Efficiency in Industries

One of the most transformative contributions of AI is its relentless drive towards innovation and efficiency across virtually all industries. Automated technologies, powered by AI, have shown the capacity to resolve complex tasks faster and more accurately than traditional human-intensive methods. Be it in healthcare, where AI assists in diagnosing diseases; in manufacturing, where it enhances operational efficiency through automation; or in the service sector, where it powers customer interaction via chatbots and virtual assistants - AI's imprint is wide and deep.

Supply chain management is another sector witnessing AI-driven transformation. By leveraging AI, organizations can anticipate and mitigate potential risks, efficiently manage inventories, streamline logistics, and optimize supply networks by using predictive analysis. Algorithms capable of analyzing copious amounts of data in real time identify performance trends, cost-drivers, and potential bottlenecks, all of which enables making informed, timely decisions.

AI's role in financial services, particularly in risk profiling, fraud detection, and trading, deserves special mention as well. AI systems are capable of identifying subtle patterns or correlations in large datasets, which would be challenging, if not impossible, for humans.

In digital marketing, AI changes the whole game with personalization. Considering individual consumer behavior and demographic data, AI delivers personalized suggestions, enhancing conversion rates and customer loyalty, thereby leading to increased profitability.

3.2. Revolutionizing Decision-making

AI, in its manifestation as Machine Learning (ML), is revolutionizing the decision-making process across sectors. ML algorithms can analyze past data patterns and applications to anticipate future scenarios. This predictive modeling capability is hugely beneficial in industries like stock trading, healthcare prognosis, or weather forecasting.

It is also equally significant in the cybersecurity industry, where ML creates predictive algorithms to detect potential cybersecurity threats and thwart attacks even before they happen. Using ML for cybersecurity risk management, as a proactive strategy, can significantly help the cyber insurance industry improve their risk profiles and make informed underwriting decisions.

Insurers can use AI applications, coupled with Big Data technologies, to evaluate potential risk factors, thereby minimizing claim ratios and optimizing premium estimates. Machine Learning algorithms analyze policyholder's data comprehensively - from their internet usage patterns and behavior to their vulnerability to specific cyber threats - hence providing a granular risk profiling.

3.3. Transforming Business Models

AI's transformative influence extends to evolving business models as well. With smart algorithms, data exchange is fast becoming a key value proposition in business models. Companies that were traditional in nature, relying on concrete products or services, now find themselves evolving into data-driven businesses.

An examination of leading businesses reveals that command over extensive data, coupled with robust AI algorithms, is fast becoming a competitive edge in the market. These systems can analyze past and present data to derive insights and forecast trends that influence strategic and daily operational decisions.

From providing personalized recommendations to customers, streamlining operations, identifying risk factors in advance to predicting market trends, AI has become a core ingredient in business modeling. Machine Learning and Deep Learning algorithms can learn from trends and make data-driven decisions that fuel economic growth, competitiveness, and innovative potential.

3.4. The Ethical and Legal Considerations

Powerful as AI is, it demands a vigilant approach to ethical and legal considerations. Questions about data privacy, security, and inherent bias seep into AI's utilization in the digital economy.

A major implication rests on data privacy and security. As AI applications need extensive data for effective functioning, businesses must ensure end-to-end safety and security of user information. Meeting these standards requires top-notch cybersecurity measures, which comes full circle to making our digital economy more secure from cyber threats.

AI can also be a double-edged sword when it involves decision-making, particularly in situations demanding complex ethical judgments. As AI algorithms are built by humans, they can carry unconscious biases, potentially leading to unfair outcomes.

Constructing mechanisms to eliminate such inherent biases remains a crucial challenge.

Further, clear legal frameworks for AI are also needed to ensure its responsible use. This includes regulating data privacy, intellectual property, and accountability, especially in case of AI making erroneous decisions impacting human lives.

3.5. Conclusion: AI's Role in Enabling Economic Growth

Despite its challenges, AI remains a critical driver of today's digital economy. It significantly contributes to the boost in productivity and efficiency of companies across sectors, all the while forging new paths for growth and innovation. Its ability to create more accurate risk profiles has considerable implications, positively influencing business decisions, individual choices, and overall market dynamics.

Moreover, AI's contribution towards enabling a more secure digital environment forms a robust layer of defense against cyber threats. This security surge becomes instrumental in shaping cyber insurance strategies and coverage planning. In the end, effectively managing the risks and leveraging the advantages of AI can make a monumental difference, bringing novel opportunities in the journey from a traditional to a digital economy.

Chapter 4. Deep Dive: Risk Assessment and AI

For any business planning to insure against cyber risk, the assessment of potential threats and vulnerabilities is crucial for defining the level of protection necessary. It is here that Artificial Intelligence (AI) steps in to reshape the landscape. Using sophisticated algorithms, AI can scrutinize vast amounts of data, identifying patterns that human analysts may miss and providing predictions on future cyber-attacks. A detailed investigation of AI's role in risk assessment will offer a comprehensive view on its influence so far and the paths toward further improvements.

4.1. AI: A Tool for Identifying Risks

The first step in the risk assessment process is to identify potential risks. Traditional approaches, while still valid, are often overwhelmed by the sheer volume of data involved in modern systems. AI can process enormous amounts of data, identifying patterns indicative of potential threats. Machine Learning (ML), a subset of AI, is particularly useful here. ML algorithms can analyze historical data, learning to predict possible future scenarios based on past events.

Identifying risks also entails understanding the attacker's methods. AI can simulate cyber-attack strategies and gauge the system's robustness against them. AI systems running these 'war-game' scenarios can enable organisations to pre-emptively strengthen weak points, thereby reducing the risk of a successful cyber attack.

4.2. Understanding Vulnerabilities

Once potential risks have been identified and categorized, the next step is to understand vulnerabilities within the system. AI, specifically ML, offers considerable advantages in vulnerability management. ML-based vulnerability scanners can crawl through an organization's systems, looking for commonly exploited weaknesses. These could include exposed sensitive data, unencrypted data transmission, or easily penetrable firewall settings.

AI systems can also anticipate 'zero-day vulnerabilities'. These are previously unidentified weaknesses which hackers may exploit before they are discovered and patched. Advanced AI systems – using predictive models – can forecast these vulnerabilities and help companies mitigate them before they are exploited.

4.3. Risk Quantification and Prioritization

After identifying risks and understanding vulnerabilities, the insurance company has to quantify and prioritize them. AI can sift through an avalanche of data and draw conclusions about the likelihood and severity of various risk scenarios. By doing so, insurers can prioritize risks, directing their focus and resources on the most significant threats.

ML-based models can embody the complex relationships between variables in cyber risk, assigning quantitative values to otherwise abstract concepts. Thus, by processing copious amounts of data and transforming them into actionable insights, AI can enable insurers to make informed decisions about risk prioritization.

4.4. Predictive Risk Modelling

Predictive risk modelling is an essential aspect of the risk assessment process. Insurers use these models to forecast potential losses in various scenarios. Here again, AI can greatly improve the accuracy and reliability of the predictions.

Advanced ML algorithms can process historical data to identify patterns that might signify a future threat. Unlike traditional statistical methods, these models can process unstructured data, incorporate new information dynamically, and constantly refine their predictions as more data is obtained.

4.5. Enhancing Transparency

AI, when used effectively, can also bring unprecedented transparency to the risk assessment process. AI's ability to process and visualize large volumes of data can provide stakeholders with deep insights into their risk landscape. This visibility can foster better communication and understanding between insurers and their clients, leading to more effective policy decisions.

However, the transparency aspect of AI calls for careful scrutiny, especially from a regulatory point of view. AI models must be designed to adhere to regulatory standards and provide clear explanations to stakeholders. Hence, the concept of 'explainable AI' is coming into focus, emphasizing the importance of developing AI models that can explain the logic behind their predictions.

4.6. The Future of AI in Risk Assessment

AI's potential in risk assessment is significant and largely untapped. As more sophisticated algorithms are developed, we can look forward to AI playing an even more influential role in identifying, understanding, and quantifying cyber risks.

However, it's essential to remember that AI is a tool, not a panacea. It performs exceptionally well when used appropriately, but it won't eliminate all cyber risks. Therefore, a balanced approach that utilizes

AI capabilities while maintaining traditional risk assessment methods is crucial.

It is also imperative to consider ethical, legal, and social issues associated with AI, such as the potential bias in AI algorithms and data privacy concerns. Incorporating these considerations will ensure that the development and application of AI in risk assessment is beneficial, inclusive, and fair for everyone involved.

In conclusion, while there are challenges to overcome, the promise of AI in enhancing the precision, efficiency, and transparency of cyber risk assessment is clear. As we witness its evolution, we can look forward to a robust and sound cyber insurance landscape that provides comprehensive coverage tailored to the unique risk profiles of organizations, thereby ensuring their safe digital journey ahead.

Chapter 5. Uncharted Territory: AI in Underwriting Cyber Policies

Artificial Intelligence (AI) has made inroads into myriad sectors, including finance and insurance. When reckoning with the domain of cyber insurance, AI displays promising potential to streamline policy underwriting processes. Let's set our explorative lens on this uncharted territory, uncovering intersections, interpreting trends, and drawing insights.

5.1. The Promise of AI in Underwriting

Insurance underwriting is an essential part of the insurance process. It involves assessing risk, setting coverage amounts, and pricing policies. The process requires a detailed analysis of information - something that AI, with its data processing capabilities, is cut out for.

With the surge in digital transitional activities, cybersecurity threats have taken a leap. Cyber insurance has consequently gained attention. When dealing with the complexity and unpredictability of cyber risks, AI can potentially revolutionize the underwriting process, aiding insurers in a more detailed, faster, and accurate risk assessment.

AI is paving an unprecedented way for underwriters through Machine Learning (ML), Natural Language Processing (NLP), and Predictive Analytics. These technologies can analyze vast and varied data sources, draw patterns, identify risk-related factors, and develop effective pricing models.

5.2. Machine Learning: Unearth the Unseen

Machine learning (ML) is a branch of AI that uses statistical techniques to provide systems the ability to 'learn' from data. For cyber insurance underwriting, ML can model a broad range of risk scenarios and unearth insights that humans might overlook.

ML algorithms can be trained on numerous cyber event datasets to predict potential risks - ranging from data breaches, ransomware attacks, to Distributed Denial of Service (DDoS) onslaughts. As the model gains more exposure to such patterns, its predictive capacity strengthens, leading to a more accurate risk assessment, further enhancing premium pricing and policy conditions.

Historical data can be combined with global cybersecurity events to build a diverse learning model which gets refined over time. ML can predict the probability of a cyber event, anticipate the magnitude of potential damage, and even suggest tailor-made mitigation strategies. This ability helps underwriters set the appropriate coverage limits and price policies accurately.

5.3. Natural Language Processing: Decipher Patterns in Chaos

Natural language processing (NLP) is another AI subset that analyzes, interprets, and manipulates human language. The adoption of NLP in underwriting cyber insurance proves advantageous in understanding unstructured data that often accompanies cyber risks.

For example, underwriters have to deal with vast expanses of text from insurance applications, risk assessment reports, emails, social media, and more. NLP can sift through this ocean of text, extracting key risk indicators and revealing patterns that humans might miss.

In the context of cyber underwriting, the adoptions of NLP can help underwriters evaluate the digital hygiene of a prospective policyholder and gauge potential vulnerabilities.

Another dimension in which NLP proves beneficial is sentiment analysis. By analyzing social media discussions, online reviews, and news articles, NLP can gauge the public sentiment towards a company's cyber risk management. This holistic analysis can notably refine the underwriting process.

5.4. Predictive Analytics: Sharpening Future Gaze

Predictive analytics involves using historical data, statistical algorithms, and machine learning techniques to identify future risks based on past patterns. Such an approach is particularly suitable in a domain like cyber security where the risk landscape rapidly evolves.

Predictive analytics allows underwriters to understand a company's potential vulnerabilities even before they lead to a breach. Parameters such as susceptibility to a specific cyber threat, past incidents, overall cyber hygiene, and industry-based risk trends, among others, can be considered.

This foresight helps in proactive risk mitigation and tailoring coverage that reflects each policyholder's unique risk profile besides guiding in pricing decisions.

5.5. Overcoming Challenges: Ethical and Regulatory Concerns

While AI presents many opportunities, it also brings about certain challenges. Regulatory and ethical concerns are at the forefront. AI models draw on vast amounts of data for predictions. This massive data processing raises critical privacy conundrums. When implemented ethically, with appropriate privacy safeguards, AI can revolutionize cyber insurance underwriting, striking a fair balance between personal privacy and data utility.

Moreover, as AI algorithms become more complex, there emerges a need for transparency and explainability. The 'black box problem', where it's unclear how AI arrived at a particular decision, may not always sit well with regulators and insurers.

In this context, embracing a 'Responsible AI' approach is crucial. It means an AI system's outcomes should be interpreted easily by humans, and the system's designing, development, and deployment should follow ethical and legal norms.

5.6. The Road Ahead

AI in cyber underwriting is proving to be a potent ally - simplifying complexities and illuminating obscure risk prospects. Enhanced risk visibility, accurate pricing, and personalized policies are consequential benefits, promoting efficiency and informed decisions.

Certainly, challenges persist - revolving around privacy, ethics, and regulations. However, appropriately addressing these can direct the trajectory towards beneficial outcomes. This exciting combination of technology, finance, and insurance invites more research, collaborations, and conversations. It's all a part of navigating this hitherto uncharted territory, as we trek towards a revolutionized insurance landscape.

In conclusion, AI has the potential to dramatically transform the way cyber insurance policies are underwritten, establishing more accurate, predictive, and personalized risk assessments. As we continue to push the boundaries, it would be fascinating to observe how these advancements in AI capabilities reflect in the realms of cyber insurance. The next few years undoubtedly hold remarkable potential and surprises, deserving our sustained attention and intrigue.

Chapter 6. Cyber threats Landscape: Identifying and Quantifying Risks

In the past decade, the landscape of cyber threats has evolved dramatically, unveiling a highly intricate network of risks expanding at an exponential pace. These risks, compounded by the rapid growth of digitalization and an interconnected global economy, pose unprecedented challenges not only to information security but also to the broader aspect of enterprise risk management.

To fully appreciate the magnitude and intricacy of these risks, it is vital first to understand the transformational shifts in the cyber threat profile and its ramifications.

6.1. The Evolution of Cyber Threats

The cyber threat of the past was primarily based on isolated incidents instigated by lone wolf hackers whose motivation was primarily experimental or intellectually driven. The threat was categorized more as a probable nuisance than a significant risk factor. However, over the years, the scenario has undergone a paradigm shift.

Today, the cyber threat model is highly sophisticated, organized, and driven by various factors ranging from financial gain, corporate espionage, socio-political ideologies to state-sponsored cyber warfare. Cyber crimes have metamorphosed from being a fringe factor to a mainstream risk element having a large scale impact on businesses worldwide.

Cyber crime has become commercialized, making it accessible to anyone willing to pay. Attackers now don't need to be technically adept; they can readily purchase off-the-shelf tools or engage professional hacking services to conduct attacks. As such, the breadth and depth of cyber attacks have expanded exponentially, making it enormously challenging to counter.

Key points concerning today's cyber threats include complex malware, state-sponsored cyber warfare, organized cyber crime, insider threats, third-party breaches, and new attack vectors like social engineering and advanced persistent threats (APTs). Each of these threats carries its unique threat profile and risk implication, demanding a tailored mitigation approach.

6.2. Identifying the Risks

One of the most effective strategies to manage cyber risk is to identify and understand the various risks inherent in your organization's business operations. These risks can be broadly categorized into technical, human, and organizational risks.

- Technical risks arise from vulnerabilities in hardware and software systems. These risks can be exploited to gain unauthorized access, disrupt operations, or orchestrate data breaches.

- Human risks stem from actions (or inactions) of employees that can lead to security vulnerabilities. These include poor password management, response to phishing emails, and inadequate awareness of security protocols.

- Organizational risks could arise from insufficient governance and management oversights or inadequate risk management practices - including outdated IT infrastructure, lack of a security culture, and deficient incident response capability.

An organization must have a risk identification strategy that addresses both strategic and operational threats, and balances between external and internal threats.

6.3. Quantifying the Risks

Quantifying the risks is a pivotal exercise in risk management. It takes into account potential loss scenarios, likelihood of occurrence, controls in place, and potential impact. The benefit of this exercise is that it transforms the often abstract concept of cyber risk into more concrete, quantifiable metrics, which can be readily understood, communicated, and acted upon.

Methodologies like risk scoring and risk rating can be employed to aggregate data and assign understandable values to the identified risks. This requires thoughtful consideration of factors influencing the potential loss severity and frequency of each identified risk.

While traditional actuarial approaches offer time-tested methodologies, the dynamic nature of cyber threats demands more forward-looking approaches. Emerging techniques like AI and machine learning can infer patterns, predict possible attack vectors, and quantify potential impact, laying the foundation for a more proactive cyber risk management approach.

6.4. Conclusion

In summary, the colossal magnitude and evolving complexity of cyber threats underscore the urgency to understand, identify, and quantify the risks associated with them, for they constitute a critical aspect of modern enterprise risk management. As the landscape continues to evolve, businesses cannot afford a static approach to risk assessment. They must seek dynamic, predictive methodologies to stay ahead of the curve.

This deep dive into cyber threat landscapes serves to illuminate some vital aspects of risk assessments and provides a realistic premise for cyber insurance coverage decisions. The comprehensive unpacking of terms, threats, and procedures is aimed at empowering you with an understanding that builds confidence and prepares you for proactive engagement with the world of cyber insurance.

Being aware of the landscape is the first step, but the journey of managing cyber risks through the right insurance coverage involves applying this understanding towards measuring your unique risk exposures and aligning them with tailored cyber insurance products.

Chapter 7. Harnessing AI to Predict Cyber Risks

As we navigate this digital age, the integration of AI in predicting cyber risks becomes increasingly pertinent. Artificial Intelligence, through its sophisticated algorithms and machine learning capabilities, has streamlined the process and enhanced accuracy in foreseeing potential cyber threats. By assimilating and processing multifaceted data from a myriad of sources, AI, in tandem with predictive analytics, empowers organizations to forecast cyber threats while tailoring insurance coverage to meet these evolving risks.

7.1. The Power of Predictive Analytics

Predictive analytics is a field driven by the power of algorithms and big data. It delves into historical and current data, identifying patterns and utilizing statistical analysis, machine learning, data mining, and modeling to predict future trends and outcomes. It formulates the basis for many AI applications, and when applied to cyber risk, offers invaluable insights.

Using AI, predictive analytics can sift through vast, intricate data sets, detect patterns, and generate predictive models. Cyber risk analytics specifically use machine learning and AI algorithms to identify cyber threats and associated risk factors, providing organizations with foresight in managing potential threats.

7.2. The Impact of Machine Learning

Machine Learning (ML), an AI's subset, autonomously learns and improves from experience. Employing ML models in cyber risk prediction have several distinct benefits. Unlike traditional statistical methods, ML algorithms can process large, complex data sets and make reliable predictions.

With its iterative nature, ML refines predictions as it interacts with new data, sharpening its accuracy over time. This feature is instrumental in predicting cyber risks as threats evolve swiftly. Traditional models may fall short as they fail to adapt or learn from new threats, whereas ML's adaptive capabilities ensure its model remains appropriate and precise.

7.3. The Advent of Deep Learning Models

Deep Learning, an advanced subset of ML, uses neural networks designed to mimic the human brain. Deep learning models are extremely adept at identifying patterns and anomalies in large data sets, making them well-suited for cyber risk detection.

These models can process unstructured, disparate data sources, such as log files, network traffic data, and user activity. Their ability to learn autonomously adds significant value in detecting anomalies and foreseeing potential threats.

7.4. Role of Natural Language Processing in Cyber Risk Prediction

Natural language processing (NLP), another branch of AI, offers unique contributions to cyber threat predictions. NLP can analyze human language in unstructured data sources (such as social media, blogs, forums) to detect activity associated with cyber threats.

Cybercriminals often use encoded language, slang, or new terms.

NLP's ability to understand and interpret human language, in its various forms, makes it instrumental in uncovering digital footprints that predict cyber threats or reveal ongoing attacks.

7.5. Case Study: AI and Threat Intelligence

A practical example of utilizing AI in predicting cyber risks involves integrating threat intelligence. AI systems can take on millions of data points from threat intelligence sources, quickly identifying risks before a cyberattack.

For instance, IBM's Watson for Cyber Security applies cognitive technology to ingest unstructured data, recognizing, interpreting patterns, and providing predictive analysis. The ability to identify threats in real-time gives companies an advantage and ample time to fortify defenses.

7.6. Application in Cyber Insurance

As AI's use in predicting cyber risks becomes more mainstream, insurance companies are leveraging these insights to inform their coverage policies. Insurers use these predictive models to quantify the risk associated with each organization, influencing rates, and coverage specifics.

Predicted cyber risks feed into liability calculations and policy premiums. When AI predicts a higher risk, the company may face higher premiums or even coverage limitations. Conversely, a company exhibiting lower risk thanks to robust cybersecurity protocols may receive more favorable terms.

7.7. Conclusion: The Future of AI in Cyber Risk

Predicting cyber risks with traditional methods becomes less effective as threats become more complex. AI's deep learning, machine learning, and NLP capabilities can leverage big data to drive more accurate, timely predictions. This data-rich, proactive strategy can significantly improve an organization's ability to protect itself.

Moreover, it holds tremendous implications for the cyber insurance industry, enabling better risk quantification, more personalized policies, and optimum pricing strategies. While we're just beginning to scratch the surface of AI's possibilities in predicting cyber risks, there's little doubt that AI will continue to influence the field in the years to come.

Chapter 8. Coverage Decisions: The AI Effect

In the hyper-dynamic domain of cyber insurance, coverage decisions cannot escape the ripple effects of technology. Central here is the burgeoning influence of Artificial Intelligence (AI). In streamlining risk analysis, facilitating consistency, and promoting efficiency, AI's multifaceted capabilities have much to offer.

8.1. AI and Coverage Determination

Essentially, coverage decisions in cyber insurance denote the process of determining whether a specific type of cyber risk is covered under a given policy. These decisions are predicated on complex risk assessment procedures. AI, with its sophisticated algorithms and machine learning capabilities, plays a significant role in shaping and influencing these decisions.

Machine learning has particularly gained prevalence in data supervision and interpretation, considerably impacting the coverage determination process. It's this technology's ability to imitate human intelligence, elevating it beyond the constraints of traditional programming paradigms, which has kindled interest. The machine learning model, by learning from vast data sets and making informed, probabilistic predictions, helps insurance providers determine which risks are best suited for coverage.

8.2. AI in Risk Identification and Categorization

Understanding risk types and categorizing them efficiently is key in coverage decision making. However, with the increasing range and variety of cyber threats, this task can be overwhelming. Enter AI, which can identify risks and categorize them based on the unique characteristics that pose a threat to a specific organization.

The AI-driven system analyzes an organization's digital architecture and identifies potential vulnerabilities, including weak cybersecurity protocols and outdated software. This forms an essential part of the coverage decision, as it allows insurers to accurately assess the threats the client may face and personalize their policy accordingly.

Moreover, AI-based models can reveal the risk correlations, allowing insurers to understand how one vulnerability can impact others, leading to cascading failures. This insight is invaluable in shaping coverage decisions.

8.3. Shifting from Reactive to Proactive Risk Management

Traditional coverage decisions have largely been reactive, addressing problems as they surface. However, the AI-driven cyber insurance landscape nudges insurers towards proactive risk management. Predictive analytics, a branch of AI, plays a critical role in this shift.

Predictive analytics harness past and real-time data to forecast potential future events. For cyber insurance, these predictions may involve identifying future risk trends, predicting likely attack vectors, and estimating potential financial impact. AI's predictive capabilities empower insurers to detect emerging risks and manage them proactively, fundamentally changing how coverage decisions are made.

8.4. Enhancing Claim Processing with AI

Developing an insurance policy is the first step; processing claims is the penultimate one, where coverage decisions are put to the test. Delays and inaccuracies in claim processing can result in financial losses for both insurer and policyholder.

AI fundamentally transforms this aspect by automating various steps within the claims process. This automation improves the speed and accuracy of claim settlement, eliminating human errors and reducing the processing time significantly. An AI-backed claim process offers detailed insights to insurers, enabling a more robust coverage decision-making strategy.

8.5. The Era of Personalized Coverage

Customized coverage is the future of cyber insurance, and AI is the cornerstone of this transformation. By analyzing data and identifying patterns, AI can help insurers offer customized coverage plans, tailored to the specific requirements and risk exposure of each client.

AI-backed telemetric data can help insurers better understand a client's cybersecurity posture, such as their network security measures, employee behavior, software updates, and more. With this knowledge in hand, insurance companies can design personalized coverage plans, fundamentally changing the way coverage decisions are made. This shift drastically reduces the chances of inadequate coverage and cultivates a more sustainable insurance ecosystem.

8.6. Mitigating Bias in Decision Making

Despite its undulating benefits, AI is not free from concerns. One notable issue is algorithmic bias, where AI models, due to biased data or design, might exhibit prejudice. Bias in AI-driven coverage decisions could lead to unfair exclusions or premiums.

The key to managing this risk lies in ensuring diversity in data, transparency in model design, and continuous monitoring for bias. Insurance providers looking to leverage AI should prioritize these aspects to ensure fair and unbiased coverage decisions.

AI continues to revolutionize coverage decision-making in the cyber insurance industry. This revolution heralds an era of efficiency, precision, and adaptability. However, as insurers ride this wave, it bears remembering that AI is a tool—robust, versatile, and powerful, but ultimately only as good as the hands and minds that wield it. AI makes the mountains of cyber insurance more navigable, but the journey is far from over. The challenge and the opportunity lie in harnessing its potential to the fullest—navigating the complex dynamic between risks and rewards, and striving for a future where cyber threats are managed accurately and comprehensively.

Chapter 9. Case Studies: AI Incorporated Cyber Insurance Success Stories

Broadly, there are four domains where AI has proven its mettle in enhancing aspects of cyber insurance - risk assessment, claims processing, policy pricing, and fraud detection. While theoretical knowledge offers its own insight, tangible case studies truly bring lessons to life. Here are a few select examples of AI's success in reshaping the dynamics of cyber insurance.

9.1. Evaluating Cyber Risks with AI: Case Study 1

A leading cyber insurance firm, CyberSure Ltd, realized the growing threat of overlapping vulnerabilities in their insured companies' digital infrastructure. To better assess this risk, the company turned to AI.

Their AI model primarily comprised machine learning algorithms for continual learning and accurate prediction. On ingesting vast quantities of historical data, AI signals were calibrated to alert on real-time deviations from identified safe patterns.

The AI's ability to spot and evaluate the whole array of vulnerabilities offered an unprecedented advantage to CyberSure. They could underwrite policies more accurately, avoiding blanket policies and instead structuring them specific to each client's unique risk profile.

The noteworthy point is how CyberSure's total claim payments dropped by 30% within the first year, largely due to the AI system's capacity to evaluate risks at a granular level and proactively advising policyholders on preventive measures.

9.2. Improving Claims Processing: Case Study 2

Aces Insure, a global insurance provider, implemented an AI model for processing claims. The sheer volume of data involved in processing cyber insurance claims amounts to numerous complex variables, making human analysis both time and resource heavy. Aces sought to expedite the process and reduce human error.

Adopting Natural Language Processing (NLP) for parsing and analyzing claims text, AI substantially improved processing time. It also helped detect anomalies or inconsistencies which might be indicative of fraudulent claims.

Post-implementation, Aces reported that their AI system accurately processed 90% of incoming claims within minutes, reducing not just processing time but also the operational expenses in the claims division.

9.3. Reining in Policy Pricing: Case Study 3

Major gains can also be acquired in the typically complex area of policy pricing. One fine illustration is DefendR Insure, a cyber insurance provider, who struggled with accurate pricing to match their clients' risk profiles.

To address this, DefendR deployed AI to analyze historical data, juxtaposed with real-time threat intelligence, effectively measuring each client's cyber risk profile. This valuable information was then mapped to personalized and dynamic premium pricing models.

The outcome was extraordinary. A 20% increase in new policy sales and a rise in renewal rates attested to the acceptance and appreciation of the more thoughtful, tailored pricing.

9.4. Detecting Fraud with AI: Case Study 4

The last case involves SecureGuard Insurance, who tackled their biggest challenge - insurance fraud. Fraudulent claims were leading to massive losses.

SecureGuard integrated their system with an AI model that adeptly detected inconsistencies or suspicious patterns in claims history and other related data. The AI also checked factors like the frequency of claims, the nature of cyber incidents reported, and the usual payout pattern.

Following AI implementation, SecureGuard registered a significant dip in fraudulent claims, with close to 90% of potential frauds detected before payout. The savings were redirected to lower premium costs for genuine policyholders, thereby strengthening client relationships.

Looking at these cases in their entirety, the common thread apart from the successful incorporation of AI, is the transformation within the companies. With AI as a partner, these cyber insurance companies could afford the luxury of swift, accurate decision making, and in doing so, elevated the entire customer experience.

Certainly, these case studies should not be viewed in isolation; instead, they merely represent the beginning of broader, more profound changes that AI could bring to cyber insurance. An understanding of AI's capabilities could influence reception and adoption, opening the way for more insurance companies to explore and invest in AI's potential. The long-term advantages are incalculable, promising a healthier insurance ecosystem.

Chapter 10. Challenges and Limitations of AI in Cyber Insurance

The advent of Artificial Intelligence (AI) in the realm of cyber insurance brings in an immense potential for accurate and efficient risk assessment and coverage decisions. However, the integration of AI into the existing infrastructure does not come without challenges and limitations. These hurdles extend across technical, ethical, and regulatory aspects, and call for substantial attention and deliberation.

10.1. Technical Challenges

AI systems, in general, demand extensive computational resources for designing, training, and testing machine learning models. Deep learning models, a subset of machine learning, are notoriously resource-intensive. While cloud-based solutions have eased computational stresses to some extent, the computational power needed for training complex models can still be prohibitive, particularly for smaller insurance organizations.

The requirement for vast amounts of data for training is another technical challenge. AI thrives on data, and the more it has, the better its performance. However, the issue lies in obtaining large, high-quality datasets that accurately represent cyber risk scenarios. Such data is often restricted due to the sensitive nature of the information involved and the presence of strict privacy and data protection regulations. On top of that, the constantly evolving nature of cyber threats makes it hard to collect complete and accurate training data.

Furthermore, the "black-box" nature of many AI systems can be problematic. While these systems can make accurate predictions, understanding exactly how they reach these decisions can be a challenge. This lack of transparency and interpretability is particularly concerning in an industry as sensitive as insurance, where outcomes of decisions may have substantial financial implications.

10.2. Ethical and Privacy Considerations

AI, particularly Machine Learning (ML), requires vast amounts of data to function effectively. Insurance companies would have to gather enormous quantities of sensitive cyber risk data from policyholders, invoking severe privacy concerns. Firms need to address these issues effectively to ensure they are not violating the privacy rights of their policyholders.

Besides, there lies the chance of intrinsic bias within AI systems, arising from the data used for training. If the data contains ingrained biases or is unrepresentative in some way, the AI system will inherit those biases, leading to discriminatory insurance practices, impacting premium calculations or claim settlements based on these biased algorithms. The impact can be far-ranging and possibly litigation-inducing.

10.3. Regulatory Challenges

The regulatory landscape for AI in insurance is murky at best. Regulators are grappling with the rapid advancements in AI and struggling to develop comprehensive regulations that cover all aspects of AI application in insurance. In many instances, existing regulations were not designed with technologies like AI in mind, leading to complexities in interpretation and application.

The lack of clear and comprehensive regulations can also generate concerns about liability. In the case of flawed or misconstrued AI predictions leading to significant financial loss, the question of who holds the responsibility becomes contentious. Is it the insurance company using the AI, the policyholder, or the AI manufacturer who is at fault? Without clear guidelines, such disputes could be tricky to resolve.

10.4. Inheriting Limitations and Future Directions

Despite AI's wonders, its application in cyber insurance bears inherent limitations. Contextual understanding, for instance, is an area where AI clearly trails humans. Cyber insurance processes often involve understanding intricate, context-rich scenarios, especially when assessing claims. AI, as it currently stands, struggles in this area.

It is important to understand these challenges and limitations within the broader context of technological progression. While AI does have its limits today, the relentless evolution of technology means that many of these challenges may be overcome in the coming years, potentially rewriting the book on cyber insurance. On this note, paramount importance should be given to continuous research and development, with a focus on improving AI robustness, efficiency, and transparency in the cyber insurance landscape.

To cope with these challenges and limitations, a cogent strategy is required that balances the adoption of AI in cyber insurance with thorough risk management protocols designed to minimize potential adverse effects. This strategy needs to be dynamic and adaptable, capable of responding to swift changes in the technology and threat landscapes. Above all, the insurance industry needs to embrace AI, not as a panacea for all issues surrounding cyber risk, but as a continually evolving tool that requires ongoing input, adjustment, and scrutiny.

Chapter 11. Future Predictions: The Road Ahead for AI in Cyber Insurance

As digital threats continue to evolve globally, the demand for cyber insurance policies grows in unison. Overlaying Artificial Intelligence (AI) on these policies presents an intriguing junction where technology and insurance intersect. AI's potential to revolutionize this nascent domain is immense, setting the stage for the future of cyber risk management and coverage.

11.1. The AI Revolution in Cyber Risk Assessment

At the cornerstone of every insurance policy lies risk assessment—a complex process involving myriad variables. Traditionally, this task has been a manual one, based on broad assumptions and statistical models. However, AI and Machine Learning (ML) have begun transforming this process, offering more nuanced, real-time risk assessments.

AI uses large sets of data to create models that can comprehend patterns and forecast future behavior. Within the context of cyber insurance, this means that AI can predict cybersecurity risks based on past data, allowing for a proactive rather than a reactive approach. It can track unfolding attack patterns, identify trends in threat actor behavior, and predict potential future attack vectors. These predictions can then inform coverage decisions, leading to more accurate, cost-effective insurance policies.

The future for AI in risk assessments is richer, more sophisticated modeling. Emphasis will be on 'predictability' rather than 'inevitability,' focusing on preventative measures as opposed to mitigating damage after-the-fact. AI-powered risk assessment may even contribute to reducing cybercrime in an indirect way—by making cyber insurance more affordable for small- and mid-sized businesses (SMBs), which might currently be underprepared for threats.

11.2. Rethinking Coverage Decisions Through AI

Another potential revolution lies within coverage decision-making. Today, coverage decisions largely depend on insurers' understanding of risk and the insured's willingness to accept certain conditions. However, AI can enhance this process in various ways.

AI's capability of handling vast amounts of data and performing in-depth analysis allows for customized risk profiling. Insurers can consider a wider range of factors and weigh them appropriately, leading to tailored policy offerings. Companies can expect bespoke policies fine-tuned to their specific risk environment, not a one-size-fits-all approach.

Furthermore, AI provides ongoing real-time monitoring, enabling adaptive coverage decisions. As the risk environment of insureds changes, so too can their insurance coverage. This dynamism allows for enhanced responsiveness to emerging threats, without a burdensome administrative overhead.

In the long term, AI's predictive powers could even result in foresight-driven coverage decisions, where insurers offer coverages for anticipated rather than historical risks. In effect, insurers could evolve from being "pay for injury" entities into "preventive" agents.

11.3. Legal and Ethical Challenges

The integration of AI into cyber insurance will inevitably raise legal and ethical issues. As AI systems lack transparency, there are concerns about accountability and bias. Moreover, the use of predictive analytics could potentially result in the risk-profiling of individuals and organizations, raising privacy concerns.

Regulatory bodies will need to develop frameworks that encourage the responsible use of AI in cyber insurance. Such frameworks might include laws about data collection, storage, and use, including provisions for handling errors in predictive models. This delicate balance between innovation and regulation is one of the key challenges facing the AI-infused cyber insurance industry of the future.

The pathway ahead offers a vista dominated by AI's potential in revolutionising the cyber insurance industry. However, much hinges on overcoming hurdles. The development of comprehensive standards and robust regulations to guide the use of AI in cyber insurance will be critical to ensure that advancements in technology are harnessed effectively, ethically, and responsibly.

Embarking on this evolutionary journey involves challenges. Yet, the potential rewards are enormous in terms of more effective risk management, cost efficiencies, and broader access to cyber insurance coverage. The momentum today points to an AI-enabled future, where navigating cyber threats is an anticipative and adaptive journey rather than a reactive one. As we hurtle towards this new horizon, it's clear that AI will play a central role in shaping the future of cyber insurance.